W9-BWG-311

European Burmese Cats

Kate Conley

**Checkerboard
Library**

An Imprint of Abdo Publishing
abdopublishing.com

abdopublishing.com

Published by Abdo Publishing, a division of ABDO, PO Box 398166, Minneapolis, MN 55439.
Copyright © 2016 by Abdo Consulting Group, Inc. International copyrights reserved in all
countries. No part of this book may be reproduced in any form without written permission from
the publisher. Checkerboard Library™ is a trademark and logo of Abdo Publishing.

Printed in the United States of America, North Mankato, Minnesota.
042015
092015

Cover Photo: Photo by Helmi Flick
Interior Photos: Photos by Helmi Flick pp. 1, 5, 17, 21; iStockphoto pp. 6, 7, 17;
    Minden Pictures p. 15; SuperStock pp. 9, 11, 13, 19

Series Coordinator: Tamara L. Britton
Editors: Tamara L. Britton, Bridget O'Brien
Art Direction: Neil Klinepier

Library of Congress Cataloging-in-Publication Data

Conley, Kate A., 1977- author.
  European Burmese cats / Kate Conley.
    pages cm. -- (Cats. Set 9)
  Includes index.
  ISBN 978-1-62403-811-2
1. Burmese cat--Juvenile literature. 2. Cat breeds--Juvenile literature. I. Title.
  SF449.B8C66 2016
  636.8'24--dc23
                        2015008835

Contents

Lions, Tigers, and Cats 4

European Burmese Cats 6

Qualities 8

Coat and Color 10

Size 12

Care 14

Feeding 16

Kittens 18

Buying a Kitten 20

Glossary 22

Websites 23

Index 24

Lions, Tigers, and Cats

Lions stalk the African plains. Tigers crouch in the jungle shadows, ready to pounce. House cats catch mice in their basements.

Though very different, all of these cats are members of the same family. The family **Felidae** includes 37 different cat species. One of these is the **domestic** cat.

About 3,500 years ago, humans began to domesticate wildcats. These cats worked as hunters. They kept mice and pests away from crops and stored food.

Today, cats have become pets. They are admired for their independence, grace, and sweetness. One beloved pet is the European Burmese cat.

The European Burmese cat

European Burmese Cats

In 1930, an American doctor named Joseph Thompson imported a cat from Burma to the United States. The cat's name was Wong Mau. Thompson believed Wong Mau was a new **breed**.

Thompson wanted to develop the breed. He thought the Siamese breed was the closest in looks and temperament to Wong Mau. So, he mated Wong Mau with a Siamese cat. Wong Mau's kittens were the first Burmese cats.

In 1949, Lilian France imported some of Wong Mau's kittens to England. France **bred** the kittens with Siamese cats. Over time, the Burmese cats in England and the United States became two separate breeds.

Today, the cats from the United States are known as Burmese. The English cats are known as European Burmese. In 2002, the **Cat Fanciers' Association** accepted the European Burmese for championship status.

The European Burmese began by breeding a Burmese cat *(far left)* and a Siamese cat *(left)*.

Qualities

European Burmese are friendly, playful cats. They love to be around people. These cats often have a favorite family member. They also enjoy spending time with other people. If this **breed** has to spend the day alone, it may become sad.

European Burmese cats enjoy lots of handling and attention. They love to sit on their owner's lap, be petted, and snuggle! These cats are also curious. They enjoy exploring, and are often in the middle of whatever their owners are doing.

The European Burmese is an intelligent cat. It can often recognize its name and will come when called. Sometimes this breed can learn commands, such as "sit" and "roll over." To keep this smart cat from getting bored, it needs toys and people or animals to play with.

The European Burmese is a healthy cat. When it is well cared for, it can live a long life. The average life span for this **breed** is between 10 and 15 years.

The European Burmese is a very affectionate and loving cat.

Coat and Color

The European Burmese has a short coat. The fur is fine and lies close to the cat's body. The coat feels silky and often looks glossy. The **breed**'s short coat requires no special care. A weekly brushing will keep the coat looking its best.

The European Burmese's coat can be a variety of solid colors. The most common colors are brown, **blue**, chocolate, **lilac**, red, and cream. The coat is often lighter in color on the cat's belly than it is on its back.

European Burmese also come in **tortoiseshell**. This color is often called tortie for short. A tortie's coat is a mix of two colors. Torties can be brown and red, blue and cream, chocolate and red, or lilac and cream.

European Burmese cats have a red gene that Burmese cats do not have. So, European Burmese have ten coat colors.

Size

The European Burmese is a medium-sized cat. An adult male usually weighs between 10 and 14 pounds (4.5 and 6 kg). Adult females are smaller. They weigh between 7 and 10 pounds (3 and 4.5 kg).

The European Burmese's head is shaped like a wedge. The top is rounded, and the ears are set far apart. The cat's eyes range from yellow to amber. The eyes are rounded on the bottom, with a slightly slanted line on the top. This **breed** has wide cheeks and a strong chin. The **muzzle** is as wide as the jaw.

The body of a European Burmese is muscular and athletic. Its chest is rounded, but the rest of its body is long and sleek. This breed's legs are long and slim. Its oval-shaped paws are small. The tail is medium length and has a rounded tip.

The female European Burmese is smaller than the male.

Care

Caring for a European Burmese begins at the veterinarian. The vet can give the cat a checkup to make sure it is healthy. He or she can also give the cat its **vaccines**. And, the vet can **spay** or **neuter** cats.

The European Burmese is a healthy **breed**. Sometimes they get **tartar** buildup on their teeth. To prevent this, owners should brush the cat's teeth with a special toothbrush and toothpaste.

The European Burmese's coat will **shed**. Regular grooming with a rubber brush will keep this under control. After brushing the coat is a good time to clean the cat's ears if needed, and to trim its claws.

Scratching is a natural behavior in cats. An indoor cat will need a scratching post. The post will keep the cat from scratching furniture and curtains!

Like its wildcat relatives, the European Burmese buries its waste. A **litter box** provides a place for the cat to do this. Remove waste from the box every day! Some cats will not use a dirty litter box.

Feeding

All cats need a balanced diet that includes meat. There are different types of cat food. These include dry, semimoist, and canned foods. Choose one that is labeled "complete and balanced." This food contains all the **nutrients** your cat needs.

Cats can be fed in one of three ways. Food can be measured out, or portion fed. It can be fed at specific times of day, or time fed. Or, food can always be available. This is called free fed. No matter how you feed your cat, make sure it always has fresh water.

Active cats such as the European Burmese will require more food than cats that like to lie around all day. However, indoor cats can easily become overweight. This can lead to health problems. So, do not feed your cat too much!

Cats lack the essential amino acid taurine. It is only found in meat. So, the active European Burmese must eat a meat-based diet to ensure good health!

Kittens

When a female European Burmese is between 7 and 12 months old, she can begin to have kittens. She is called a queen. Once the queen has mated, she is **pregnant** for about 65 days. Then she delivers her kittens. On average, there are four kittens in a **litter**.

Newborn kittens are helpless. They cannot see or hear until they are 10 to 12 days old. The mother cat cares for her kittens. The kittens drink their mother's milk, and stay close to her to keep warm and safe.

It is important for kittens to stay with their mother. The mother cat teaches her kittens how to be cats. She shows them how to groom, hunt, and act around people. When European Burmese kittens are between 12 and 16 weeks old, they are old enough to leave their mothers. They can be adopted by a loving family.

This European Burmese kitten has a chocolate coat.

Buying a Kitten

Adopting a kitten is a big decision. If you decide to bring home a European Burmese cat, find a reputable **breeder**. Good breeders know the history of their cats. They sell healthy, **socialized** cats that have had **vaccines**.

When buying a kitten, check closely to make sure it is healthy. Its ears, nose, mouth, and coat should be clean. The eyes should be bright and clear. The kitten should be alert and interested in its surroundings.

Before bringing home your new pet, be sure to get some supplies. Food and water dishes, food, and a **litter box** are the most important items to have on hand. The veterinarian can recommend a good kitten food. It has all the **nutrients** a growing kitten needs for a long, healthy life.

The European Burmese is an uncommon cat. Kittens may be difficult to find. The search will be worth it!

Glossary

blue - a coat color that is bluish gray.

breed - a group of animals sharing the same ancestors and appearance. A breeder is a person who raises animals. Raising animals is often called breeding them.

Cat Fanciers' Association - a group that sets the standards for judging all breeds of cats.

domestic - tame, especially relating to animals.

Felidae (FEHL-uh-dee) - the scientific Latin name for the cat family. Members of this family are called felids. They include lions, tigers, leopards, jaguars, cougars, wildcats, lynx, cheetahs, and domestic cats.

lilac - a coat color that is pinkish gray.

litter - all of the kittens born at one time to a mother cat.

litter box - a box filled with cat litter, which is similar to sand. Cats use litter boxes to bury their waste.

muzzle - an animal's nose and jaws.

neuter (NOO-tuhr) - to remove a male animal's reproductive glands.

nutrient - a substance found in food and used in the body. It promotes growth, maintenance, and repair.

pregnant - having one or more babies growing within the body.

shed - to cast off hair, feathers, skin, or other coverings or parts by a natural process.

socialize - to adapt an animal to behaving properly around people or other animals in various settings.

spay - to remove a female animal's reproductive organs.

tartar - a hard, yellowish crust that forms on teeth when saliva acts on food particles.

tortoiseshell - a coat featuring patches of black, orange, and cream.

vaccine (vak-SEEN) - a shot given to prevent illness or disease.

Websites

To learn more about Cats,
visit **booklinks.abdopublishing.com**. These links are routinely
monitored and updated to provide the most current information available.

Index

A

adoption 18, 20

B

body 10, 12
breeder 20
Burma 6
Burmese 6, 7

C

care 14, 15, 16
Cat Fanciers' Association 7
character 8
claws 14
coat 10, 14, 20
color 10, 12

E

ears 12, 14, 20
England 7
eyes 12, 20

F

Felidae (family) 4
food 16, 18, 20
France, Lilian 7

G

grooming 10, 14, 18

H

head 12
health 9, 14, 16, 20
history 4, 6, 7
hunting 4, 18

K

kittens 18

L

legs 12
life span 9
litter box 15, 20

M

muzzle 12

N

neuter 14
nose 20

P

paws 12

R

reproduction 18

S

scratching post 14
senses 18
shedding 14
size 12
socialization 18, 20
spay 14

T

tail 12
teeth 14
Thompson, Joseph 6
toys 8

U

United States 6, 7

V

vaccines 14, 20
veterinarian 14, 20

W

water 16, 20
Wong Mau 6, 7